WATERCOLOR PASTEL

12 SHEETS SINGLE-SIDED
SCRAPBOOKING DESIGNS FOR CRAFTS

SCRAPBOOK PAPER PAD
6x6, NON-PERFORATED SHEETS

© Crafty As Ever

To remove cut along the dotted line.

To remove cut along the dotted line.

To remove cut along the dotted line.